Other books by
Stewart S. Warren

~~~~~~

Shape of a Hill

The Weight of Dusk

Second Light

The Song of It:
A Travelogue of Norteño

Essence:
contemplations in image and word
with Corinna Stoeffl

The Sea Always Near

Just One Leaf

Mercury HeartLink
www.heartlink.com

Stewart S. Warren

Just One Leaf

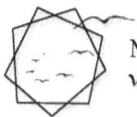

Mercury HeartLink
www.heartlink.com

Contents

One Storm Follows Another

A Gypsy in Time

Hunting Down Death

I Say, Let Them Live

A Soft Halleluiah

We are, all of us,
of the same origin,
the same blood.

Then... for family.

INTRODUCTION

If you scratch the Hill Country of Texas it's nothing but limestone. Shell white under dusty green—a giant water filter. I had stopped along a ranch to market road east of Comfort to photograph a gathering of Daddy Long Legs in the cool recess of a limestone overhang. They were thick as hay and stretched for over twenty feet. When I reached my arm in they moved as one, like sardines in school, a dark hoary being living peacefully under the soft rock. After a few attempts to capture that likeness of spider mass I got back in my Ford station wagon V-8 and went on down the road. It was an older car and preferred gentle suggestions as to which way it should go, then, after some lag time it would veer in that general direction. I continued drifting east toward Kendalia.

The country rose and fell like the sea that had formed it. Juniper (called Cedar by many) dominated the scene except where the land had been cleared for cattle, or down in deeper canyons where ancient Cypress sank their wing-like roots into the water. Cedar breaks and open meadows—open, closed, open. Gently up, gentle down, with clear rivulets that all headed to the Guadalupe River, to Aransas Pass, the Gulf of Mexico. Coming over a small rise I settled into some bottom land, a stand of scrub oak on my right, a clearing on my left. There, in the open meadow stood six or seven Native Americans. They were spread out ten to fifteen feet apart, and were finely dressed as if attending a naming ceremony, a social dance, or the signing of treaty in a place more friendly to their nation than Texas.

I was three years sober and on my way back from a 12 Step convention in Kerrville. It was 1985. In my estimation I had not engaged in a very lively way with Native America. Oh, sure, shortly before I sobered up I had taken an interest in certain teachings, had devoured God Is Red by Vine Deloria, Jr., and even some Sun Bear. I took a circular kitchen clock off the wall once and painted over the gratuitous French chicken with a turquoise background and laid out the four colors of the cardinal directions, but that didn't constitute an area of study. And in 1979 I had participated in the building of a sweat lodge along the banks of a stream near Alpine, Arizona and had my first taste of strict traditional ceremony from a man who had just returned from Pine Ridge.

But forays into different teachings are not unusual in my life. At any given moment I might take up a self-paced and often self-directed study of any path that speaks to me. Sacred Geometry (which allowed me to develop my "logo"), the pyramids of Egypt, archeology of the Southwest and Astronomy are on that list. In the mid '80s a vision of American Indians, however, was not part of my curriculum—not consciously anyway. Clearing away the wreckage of my past so that I might find a Power by which I could live was the path I was on at that time. It was spiritual but simple: get your ego and suffering in check, or die. The relief from not poisoning myself with alcohol was tremendous; the camara-derie and community was an incredible bonus. Gratitude is not an option for me, it's a privilege.

Four years later I did hook up for a while with a group of sober non-natives, most of them good people, who were learning native ways: ceremonies, traditions, lifestyle. Among other things we were putting one another "out on our blankets" as an initiation and a coming of age in the old ways. We were on Vision Quest. I recounted the story of the vision I'm about to tell you, but they were less than impressed. They were having way too much fun, as was I for a while, messing around with what a friend called a lot of "dead stuff," flesh, feathers, skulls and such. Besides, skipping grades was not allowed in their school and they were more interested in flesh offerings.

As the station wagon floated down into the draw and I saw the "teachers," feathered and robed, I heard a strong, clear voice. It sounded like someone was riding in the backseat and had just leaned forward to speak into my ear. The genderless voice said, "Stewart, you're not a traitor! Remember, we sent you to live with the white man." I immediately began sobbing, uncontrollably, as they say. I was able to pull the car over to the side of road opposite the field of Indians, where I continued to cry, though I didn't really know why. It was as though a huge question had been answered that I didn't know I had asked. It was major pieces of the puzzle put into place. But what puzzle?

When I wiped my eyes enough to look to the left, the field was empty—no Native Americans, no family, no teachers. I did see, however, that where they stood were tree stumps cut closely to the ground to allow for grazing. The stumps were gray and rotting into the earth. On my right, through the open window, was a herd of Hill Country Deer. Maybe a dozen or so. They had come down close to the car and were making a grunting noise that sounded like grinding their teeth with their mouths closed. We looked at one another as they moved among the small oaks. I had no particular thoughts about that event and no other information was forthcoming. I started my car and went back to Austin.

There is no conclusion here, no sacred bundle tied with horse hair, no Ah-Ha that gives us the reason, meaning and purpose to the author's life. Shucks. But readers of my work will have noticed, or, you are about to notice, references and perspectives that seem to be native. But hey, I have references to modern astronomy, evolutionary process and even Voo Doo, so what's up with that? I use anything at hand to further my experience and evolution. And for all the efforts of my life—the posturing, instigating and migrating to and fro—the resulting contributions have been miniscule in the face of what's needed in the world, though I would have hoped otherwise. And so would my family.

My expectations have always been a great deal more grand than my actual deeds, writing included. That's just the way it's been. And whether I have alluded myself once again or am closer to something real for myself, I come back to that vision in the Hill Country when considering my place in the world. I see myself as a reporter, a scout. My job is to witness, to observe this culture, this western wave of humanity. After all, they didn't tell me to go "do" something about it.

In the poem *Why I Live in Town*, that appears in <u>Shape of a Hill</u>, I wrote: "And a poet, though his or her hands are often bound, must be made to witness everything." If I'd have listened to my own words I might have saved myself some angst. In truth, I've wrestled the world within myself and drug a number of people through my attempts to "correct" society. I've been a pain in the ass. My arrogance in assuming that I've known what's best, along with my general aloofness when it comes to relating to people has made it difficult to be close. And, as a friend dealing with a serious health challenge said, "I'm going to live until I die." So, I have an undetermined, yet finite amount of time to truly surrender to the love I talk so much about. Fortunately, my clay feet are rapidly dissolving in a flash flood that's too wide to skirt—thank God.

Perhaps it would have been easier for me to get my cues, as most people seem to do, from so-called external sources. But life has taken pity on my debilitating shyness. I get stuff in dreams, meditations, messengers riding shotgun. And it helps to have a sense of humor about all this. Last year I had a series of lucid dreams in which I would "wake up" in a dream and direct its course for what seemed a brief flicker of time. *"Hey, I'm walking around in a dream. I think I'll try flying."* That sort of thing.

In one dream I found myself standing at a podium addressing an audience. I "woke" and realized the body was asleep in my bed somewhere and that I could make choices, do things. I looked out onto an almost empty hall with just a few people on the back row. I thought, lucidly, *Wow, what would I like to do?* Instantly, I heard myself shout, "I WANT TO MEET JESUS!" Nothing happened. Nor has anything I can connect with that event happened since. See what I mean about having a sense of humor?

Earlier this year, after the publication of <u>Essence</u> with Corinna Stoeffl but before I put together <u>The Sea Always Near</u>, I had another type of dream. It was one of those nights when mortality comes creeping around, sniffing at your door just for grins. This time the pressure in my chest and shooting pains up to my ears went on for quite a while. I took aspirin, got back to sleep, woke with more pain, slipped off again into restless slumber. Then I had this dream. Actually it was a dialogue while the body slept. I came into the event saying, to someone or to some thing, "So, you're not actually saying that you're going to take my life, but rather that I've nothing left to do, no more tasks in the world—is that correct?" My question was confirmed and I went on to ask a couple more. I put a bit more expanded version of the conversation into one of my poems.

The relief and joy of this communication was immense, the double helix of yellow-green light convincing. But later, when I put my clever *little mind* on the case, I found objection. But, but, but, what do you mean? What the fuck have "I" accomplished... "I" haven't done enough? [Just here to witness, remember?]

Are these poems my witnessing? I'm not sure, or, umm... I don't think so. I suspect that outside of the time/space which is this world, that the reporting has, is, already being done. As for all this scribing and poem-making, *I can't not do it.* Or it feels that way. Who knows, maybe writing just helps keep me off the streets and out of jail, but I want it to *mean* more than that. At first the writing of poetry afforded me a vehicle for getting to know the themes of my life, for checking in on my process and progress.

And it still does. Writing keeps me connected to something truer than the daily drama and shared construct we keep projecting. I could also say now that it's a way for me to postpone my leaving, keep the relationship going. It's okay to be exhausted by love.

Recently I feel as though I'm taking one last good look, and, as usual, my words fall incredibly short at describing what I see, what I know. The beauty of this world, suffering and all, is heart breaking and heart rendering. The wonder of it is beyond anything I can convey—though I try. I can't touch the big stuff like some artist do, but I invite you to look with me, in awe if you will, at the miracle of life on this blue green jewel, the miracle of just one leaf. Just one!

—Stewart S. Warren, Albuquerque, NM, 2010

Ken Gurney

0423

like = must
as soon??

They tell me that in the future
we'll be better equipped for work.
Well, you tell 'em for this

if I could ever vote, I would never vote
for no says got area on its mind.

→ [last verse]

(gold awnings, only color---)

We'll make markers for our own.
the still across the sloping field and —
down in the trampled corn the stalk
is starting to rise. ——→

Suffrage

They pulled up the fence posts for the wounded,
wrestled the boys in and out, tore
the canvas up or watered and used it
to cool the cannons, rinse the surgeons' hands.
The Civil War, they say, the Civil War
was full of color. The blue coats
of the fallen, the gray of the Rebels,
red in both flags, red soaking into the
ground, red when the cannons overheated,
red screaming through my dreams;
(a burst of white, orange at night)
it's always dark when the fire is done.

This morning its our turn to bury
the dead — our side won the battle?
I look for my husband, my brothers,
my sister's boy. I roll them over
whether they're breathing or not.
Either way, I gotta tend to

Yesterday the cannons took all the troops,
the able and the faltering, chased the enemy
across the river. Just us camp followers left.
Still the mighty shatter of war to the other side
the same old story in the river —
The crows and the blackbirds and the hogs
already starting in on the ones left for dead.

One Storm Follows Another

A New Mexican Landscape

I'm undone once again—
the way the blue lays soft,
lays down, lays hot
along the running peaks and saddles
of the Sangre de Cristos, the two
disappearing at the known edge.

It's none of our business
what happens after that—not yet.

This is the same blue curve
of her dress open under the arm,
a stitched hem laying easy
against warm flesh, that intersection
of arm and shoulder and breast
inviting the press of fingers,
the investigation of chin.

But first a smile, the code
that unlocks this land.
How it makes crinkles
at the edges of her eyes, how
that string of pearls ignites.

Each wide green leaf
is a hand, something good to eat,
to hold against your cheek.
    There's no denying her breath.

She pulls me in, close,
and for the millionth time this moment
I explode into the raw roots
of what is visible, what is
    quivering, juicy, willing
to be made into a sun-struck day.

HEART OF BROTHERS

Half an hour down, twice that
coming up. The Rio Grande
did not cut this gorge.

The water found it
after the molten crust of earth
cooled and pulled apart, but before
saber tooth and scimitar cats
sprang into extinction,
    before we made our plans
to hike down to Big Arsenic Springs.

A six hundred and eighty foot descent
switch-backs the canyon wall,
calls for pause, for encounters.
Lichen, Penstemon, Steller's Jays,
crush of aromatic herbs,
varieties of Artemisia.
As the day warmed and the sap ran
    we leaned into Ponderosa,
smelled that natural Butterscotch.

Pictographs are painted on stone,

petro glyphs are pecked into rock.
We followed herds of Big Horn Sheep
running across Basalt, a spaceman
    pointing True North.
My brother who is Turtle Heart,
    but for the day I called Big Otter,
was drawn to the correction of water.
We made our way through boulders
to shore, summer grasses bent in a bowl
where deer might have slept.

Here the spring gabbled
over watercress gardens, spread
cool and clear into the wild river.
All along the Rio Grande Uplift
arsenic is common in ancient aquifers,
smaller amounts curative, medicinal.
    We were there for the healing,

wasted no time shedding hats,
shirts, wallets. After all,
we'd come a long way: marriages, tornadoes,
jobs, no jobs, scars on our hearts and bellies,
impending doom, alcoholism,
    the stuff of childhood
that takes a lifetime to reckon,
the usual wounds of the world.

The river knew what to do.

We slipped in, eyes just above water,
pawed to a big rock in the middle.
    See what I mean about Otter?
I could hear my brother's heart
ticking, ticking, lining up
with the current. Feet first

is how we did faster moving water,
rolled onto our backs the canyon
    above us was Heaven,
    the river pure Creation,
waves over rock big as bears shouldering us—
smooth, black, determined.

Higher up the bank
we saw long deep gouges in stone
where river-tumbled boulders
had been driven, smashed, carried.
    The river has no patience;
the life it delivers knows no hesitation.
This is the wild river we've always run,
    the shared torrent of becoming,
the unbreakable heart of brothers.

Beautiful Thought, Beautiful View

I.

I just stood there
waiting for the body
to do something, for *it*
    to know what was next;
fluff the filter in the cone,
grind the beans, make the call.

But no, nothing was happening—
for an instant the mind-body
was blank, on pause.

And if it hadn't rebooted itself
I might have stood there
for days, a cow sleeping standing.
What happens, or doesn't, in that moment?
    Who doesn't do?

If this blip in time were a door
perhaps I could have woken up there,
    standing in a dream, then,
gone on about the business of designing creation.

II.

Song of the children splashing,
the eager green vine
and flow of holy ice,
    I bring all of you into me
as a whale swallowing the sea.
I remember our days of fire,
our water making.

All my friends—creatures
that swim and roam and fly,
that blink and see, that migrate
as continents, that move
as currents and seeds
blown on the wind—all of you—
    I thank you, and
I call you into council.

Because of you and for
the Great Morning Glory
opening into its own light and time
    I stand and I see, and I am
now ready to create.
How shall we proceed?

III.

When I speak
I speak for the crest of the wave.
If not me, then who?
How shall I arrive?

I will come
in the exchange of green,
the conversation of blue,
    the power of a single drop
of water. I will come

thrusting as a mountain,
whispering as silence, roaring
as a star, as human.

Everything in you is behind you.

From this moment on
    look in, then, look out;
beautiful thought,
    brilliant beautiful view.

BERNALILLO

With the late sun
lighting the tops of cottonwoods,
their massive limbs curving slow in ¾ time
extending leafy shrouds bigger than houses,
and farmers in rubber boots
turning sluice gates on their way home,
    I enter Bernalillo Valley from the south,
between the river and the rails.

The green farms and wooded lowlands
release their bouquet of glover hay,
the underworld of rotting ravines.
    Horses, goats, trash fires, cemeteries,
the dark earth of past civilizations.

And though you see politics of conquerors—
of the haves and of those who were had—
    being chiseled anew
into the *retablos* of our outer lives,
tonight we settle down together
in the cooling air of the Bosque.

Cows repose next to their neighbors;

field birds rise one last time, shake out,
sink into the abating earth. Owls lift
as silhouettes into the orange band of western sky.
I kick across the dusty road, El Camino Real,
to find dinner in the old village.

Whatever we have or think we have;
whatever was rent from the land
or ruined within us, the sharpening of knives
and the bleating of lambs, settles
    in the softness of grudges set aside;
the evening sky taking trouble from us.

Inside, the clatter of voices and dishes,
the smell of the skillet and pot,
families passing salt across tables,
and two young women with guitars in the bar
singing songs of the folly of separation.
    I could have ordered fast food in the city.

On my way home I circle through Corrales,
the river again on my left,
tunnel of overhanging branches,
intoxication of those teeny white flowers
that bloom only at night—
the Moon, Venus, other invitations.

At Dusk

At dusk the day is closer, but slipping,
a song with violin solos between verses,
butterflies choosing their last leaf.
Her sweaty hair is pushed off her brow
    after digging the garden
and slinging kids on and off her hip.
The mountain, always at one shoulder,
is letting go in a slow lavender sigh.

She's been speaking to that mountain all day
in the silent currents of her arms and thighs.
She speaks as a lover without manners,
the same way she talks to the ocean
hundreds of miles away.
She hears the sea rolling high in the clouds;
she sees everything sinking beneath it;
    she wants to go home
but her children aren't ready for the journey.

When her man arrives he's full of the sun,
of machinery noise and flat-footed thinking,
of storms coming up sudden, and strong talk
about who's not doing their job.

He's looking for a landing,
for a place to unload, let darkness finally fall.
He smells of road dust and sharpened steel,
of salt and wind and hidden regret.
   He's hungry.

At dusk his hours grow shorter.
At dusk her shadows grow longer.

He's worked all day from one end of the field
to the other and still
everything leans forward, the next day
pressing like a list. He thinks:
everything within sight should be within reach.
He looks proudly at his children and says,
Don't worry, I'll fight 'til I win.

The mountain is silent now
marked only by missing stars.
It's larger than ever and she lets it hold her,
guiding her life like a dancer.
Her world goes backward and forward,
goes to the village of her mother
   and to the children of her children.
Her world turns with the ocean.

At dusk he stumbles

over the last sand hill and comes
   to the shore of her,
to the running waves crashing,
grateful, exhausted, finished.

Good Thyme Café, Canon City, Colorado

At 410 Main Street
the cooler has quit in the kitchen
and Caelyn waits tables one hot plate at a time.
A barn wood wainscot runs around the wall
with a garland of plastic Spruce boughs,
twinkle lights woven through them,
an occasional cluster of dusty flowers.
From there on up
it's framed photographs and paintings
    as high as a hammer can ring, then
the painted tin ceiling.

Photographs of snowy ranges, roses,
driftwood and chain lightning
sit side by side with little cards
that tell us what we're looking at, the locations.
    But the paintings are mute
and viewers must add their own poetics.
Hanging on the wall of the men's room,
and just above the john, a likeness
of a solemn buffalo standing.

Four blocks west a territorial prison

built in 1871 against a sheer rock bluff
is busy with the work of corrections.
Balancing delicate as razor wire an angel
tiptoes along the ridge of the south wall.
At her right hand cottonwood leaves
toothed and wide shower from twigs,
the green grass of summer far below;
on her left a scene we can only imagine.
    No Photographs Allowed.

Some say that edges are harder here:
stainless steel commodes,
barked commands, concrete floors,
postal regulations, the clock.
But some things are easy to get:
sex, needles, television, semi-private rooms,
syndication, folded laundry, lawyer talk;
    same as on the street,
though a sunset is hard to come by.

In the morning someone's up early
cooking the rice, boiling the coffee.
Cows in the barn turn a wary eye.
Someone on their bunk reads
quietly to themselves.
In eight minutes Hell will arrive.

Whatever deals were made
(with or without consent)
paying up is what turns the day.
Commerce. Commerce. Commerce.
You have to play to win;
    and, you have to play. Like I said,
    same as the street.

Out on the irrigation gang someone looses
a finger while a guard looks the other way;
a friend comforts a friend standing in line;
a package arrives.
At night, just after lights,
a girl who used to be a boy
sings a lullaby and puts the men to sleep.
Someone thinks hard
    about what they've done, thinks
there's some good and bad in everyone.
Kindnesses must come disguised
as small gestures; a knife
can sometimes tell the truth.

Dream big, but dream to yourself;
that angel knows your name.
Back at the Good Thyme Café she's waiting tables—
19 more months and 3 more days.

SILVA'S SALOON, ENDANGERED
for outlaws, past and ever so present

They've given death a name
and now they're going to cure it.
They're burning out our homesteads
and hiding places, anything
made of iron, dirt, honest grief
        and straight words.

They can kill in the dark
from a thousand miles away,
a video game that simulates blood splatter,
        while real live babies
lose arms, real live legs.

At Silva's Saloon every artifact
has handprints: hats, trophies, photographs.
Those bare breasted girls watching
from oil paintings behind the bar
soothe the pain, help
to unravel the barbed wire.

North of the pool table
there's a creak in the floor—

surveillance satellites are searching for it.
Everything with a crack is suspect,
    and everything has one.

Kell and Kendall sing the windmill songs;
songs of the high lonesome,
the whine of the wire, the shared load,
carrots just out of the ground.

Sing now cowboys, sing
of forgiveness—the high plains kind
    that can level churches
to the rubble of their pretensions.

If it weren't for those nudes on the wall
we might hand over the poetry
    and let 'em take us
without a revolution.

Confession

*March 18, 2010 marks the 20th year that frames hang
empty at the Isabella Stewart Gardner Museum as a
reminder of the theft of thirteen works of art taken from
its galleries. The frames hang empty today as an homage to
the missing artworks and as a placeholder for their return.*

I could have stolen those paintings
in fifteen minutes, all of them,
the Degas, the Rembrandts, even the Vermeer.
Dressed as two Boston cops,
I stashed the security guards
in the basement, had the joint
all to myself, hung around for two more hours
    but could have done it in fifteen.

Reports flew in, informants squawked,
everybody claimed a piece of the pie.
Like pigeons they flapped
from plot to plot, like pigeons
they followed their own crumbs.

Irish Boston tried to gesso it's tarnished pride,
the papers hung everybody out to dry.

Underworld characters top to bottom
said this is about money
        and mostly power, muttering
in their beer, beneath their love.

Some fiend sent chips
of Seventeenth Century paint, like fingers
of hostages they arrived in a vial.
But that's not my style.
And the art world, Oh, my God!,
tears in their eyes, a sigh in their hearts.
"These works of art should be available
        to everyone, children to come,"
but just how public should a collection be?
I could have done it in fifteen.

I could have lifted the entire museum,
three stories of Venetian façade, courtyards
full of the female figure in marble,
        but it took light years to get here.
I come from a world
you can't yet imagine, a star system
in the Perseus arm of our galaxy.

Call me a thief, but I'm a traveller—
a curator and admirer of humanity.

These dreams you dream: tragic,
heartbreaking, sublime;
call them gardens, call them cities,
call them sculptures and paintings,
they're always destroyed
at your own guilty hand, ruined—
    so I've saved thirteen for posterity,
for the children light enough
to lift into the starry wind,
bright enough to shine their way
past the shoulder of Orion.

Your children will want to know
where they came from: faces
like pearls, a lilting hand
moving with the music of creation,
    that bright red chair.

As for the rest, I will tell them
all that I saw that night
of your determined journey,
    your blossom of hope,
the masterpiece that is
your storm and your concert.
    I will tell them of a love
that even I could not embrace
in a mere fifteen minutes.

The Root and the Pot
from Craig Child's Finders Keepers

We assume it travels in darkness.
But what do we know
of the underground? The moment
we break the surface with plow
or dynamite or trowel the daylight
of our world rushes in.

A ceramic pot goes to die.
It's laid to rest in a ceremonial chamber;
left and never reclaimed
in a cache high in a cliff;
abandoned abruptly on a kitchen floor
for terrible reasons, unavoidable consequence.

The journey is slow—
    one dust storm at a time,
    collapse of rock shelf,
    layer of volcanic ash.
The black swirls and lines
are a barcode of infinite data,
    but the lips say everything.
So begins the afterlife of a pot.

North of the ecliptic
between White House and Wupatki
summer students crouch
in trenches with flags, tags, notebooks,
canteens, finger picks and dusters—
treasure hunters all grown up,
    the sophistication of Archeology.
We aren't grave robbers.

All afternoon (an eighth of an inch at a time)
she works to loosen
the pot from its tomb.
A juniper root found it first,
    finders keepers, so now
she must wrestle it gingerly
    from dirt *and tree.*
Already cracked by seeking fingers,
it comes apart in her hands.
The notes she makes
provide attempts at cultural context,
    create stories for museums,
distance her from shame.

When she's done a hollowness is left
where juniper hands once held
the roundness of relationship.

With a cross-cut saw
she hacks off the probing root.

At night, after canvas tarps
have been tethered with rocks
across the labyrinth of trenches,
and a walkway of cold stars
    wipes the sky from east to west,
a lone juniper remembers its hand,
a stump hanging in space.

In a plastic bag, in a cardboard box,
in the back of a van, pieces
of naked pottery like cheekbones
shudder in disturbed death.

ONE STORM FOLLOWS ANOTHER

"Just drive me around," he says,
"see if any of my friends are still livin'."

This is her mom's dad from Black Mountain.
If no one drives him around the res
he'll get on the road and start hitch-hiking.
No one wants to see this;
he'll be a hundred in December.

"Go this way," he motions
up an old mining road.
When she makes the turn
beadwork and feathers slap the windshield;
the jolt tries to throw him
but he sits the saddle well.

She's as good on the back roads
as she is at rush hour in Albuquerque.
These are her roots; these
are the red rock hills that heave
and whisper in her dreams;
this is the hour with no face,
    the familiar road lifting into the sky.

He tells her stories about working
the mines; working the gas fields;
    the dog food handouts;
sheep-bewildering fences;
movies he made with John Wayne.
"We always played the savages."

But this is not what he came to tell her.
Sure, these stories are part of every feast,
    every famine. She knows them
like skin, like the sound of her own breathing.
This is her talking, her hearing the timbers crack,
being forced to grab a jammed pump jack,
faking her own death over and over.

"Stop here,"
he says, as they break through
juniper onto the mesa top.
From this high rock distant lands
go orange through fuchsia to purple;
below, a sparse constellation of hogans,
a riderless horse, a horseless rider;
the goodbye sun speaking that one word.

"Listen, my granddaughter,
even our own good songs
will be thrown aside, torn by the wind."

"This is disagreeable, hard to accept.
But it is also true for the ones
who keep pushing us to the edge,
who try to contaminate our mind."

"One storm follows another," he says,
"there is only one good way out of here.
    Hold on to your heart,
let everything else fall beneath you."

A silhouette of power lines
from a coal-fired power plant
struts across the horizon; behind that
the tall walking rain leans south,
    turns, sweeps north;
behind that the blue bowl of sky
dies into a mind of stars—
one world after another.

They share a silence without length;
the valley is lost in one shadow;
the day gives itself to night.

Without turning he says,
"Let's go to the house now, see
if they saved us something to eat."

A Gypsy in Time

This Dream that Yearns to Move On

Sweet presence of planet, your life passes
from stone to stone, a flower
seeking a perfect range of conditions,
a thought following the sun
through a string of pearls.

At the trailing edge: decay;
at the leading edge: an idea;
as with the word, never an end.

A gypsy in time, you twirl,
a face always half in shadow,
a woman on her fourth marriage—
wise, weary, still so fertile,
more beautiful than ever.

I suckle on the slope
of your mountains, eat from your hand,
drill like a long-beaked bird
to taste the varieties of your nectar.
I sow and I reap—
I am, after all,
the blush of your will.

THE SHIP THEY COULDN'T SEE

There's that story again—
the one about indigenous islanders,
Aztecs and Incas, how
they couldn't see the ships
rising on the horizon, coming
straight at them. Unfathomable.
But who was it that couldn't see?

Towering cities hewn of shining stone,
shoulder to shoulder citizens
for a thousand miles, villages
like lily pads; you could step
from one to another and never fall in.
A conqueror must ignore many things.

People who burden beasts to carry
their load on sleds made with wheels
    arrived on the shores of mystery
and saw only, "no wheels."
While interlocking wheels of higher math,
calendars made of precious yellow metal
extended far into time
(and therefore space),

a journey across millennium,
    but these wheels didn't count.
Let's melt the gold and eat it!

There was another roundness
that couldn't be seen—the zero—
not only for counting higher
but for negative numbers, multiplication too.
So baffling, hard to see, these bright
feathered heathens that need subduing.

Sponsoring agents back in the offices
of Lisbon, Madrid and The Vatican
were glad to hear of endless virgin lands
open to expansion, up for grabs.

Since no one lives there—
no one of consequence—
we'll confuse them
with the written word.
By the authority of God
    we can do anything we please
with bibles, horses, steel.

When the newcomers arrived
they shed their shirts of animal hide and metal,
preferred the lighter, softer touch of native

cotton, something they could feel.
But more subtle touch
eluded *Los Conquistadores.*
  The Inca used woven cord
for archival purposes, talking threads.

Strings hanging from a central cord,
each with a myriad of precise knots,
choice of textures, twenty four colors,
distance between intersections,
decisions about types of tying.
They read them with their hands—
  a system of communication
equaling that of Europe.
No written language, indeed!
We see what we want to see.

Here's how you conquer a continent:
bring a series of diseases
for which your opponent has
not developed the DNA,
  wipe out nine tenths of the population
and make the weakened survivors
kneel before the king's sword.
  It's true, the Small Pox
was a ship they couldn't see.

THE CLATTER OF A COUNTRY

She stood up in the middle of lunch
at a restaurant full of 4-tops, buttresses
of high booths lining the walls,
every seat claimed by a diner.
"I don't know any of you," she announced,
    "I feel alone."

Faces turned, forks dropped,
waiters froze—for just a moment—
then all returned to being
the restaurant they were dreaming.
Chatter, chatter. Clatter, clatter.
    More pie, please.

But one by one, and sometimes
as a mission of two,
good people came quietly over
and dropped off solutions:
more bread, stacks of dessert,
magazines back to front, a case
of cell phones, religious pamphlets,
downloads, online subscriptions,
    instructions on how to vote, even

the wine list, GPS, lip gloss, a puppy.

She ate everything she was handed;
used cream pie to swallow the phones;
rolled up a magazine to get the dog down;
slathered on makeup, licked it off.

A woman corrected her
about her use of prayer but let her be
when she wolfed down the phone book.
Finished, she napkined her lips,
tipped the server, started her car.

Next day the newspapers covered her demise.
That afternoon she had boarded a plane
headed for Extinction
that exploded over a country
called The United States of America.
    Now a celebrated victim of not enough,
you see shrines to her tragedy in every household.
    Everyone fears her story.
They deliver truckloads of distraction
to appease her ghost.

When they eat, they throw up
so they can keep on consuming.

THE DREAM OF PUPPETS

From the description of Randa Mdah's sculpture by John
Berger in his introduction to Mural *by Mahmoud Darwish*

I know the dream of puppets, the one
with the audience that's made of paper mâché,
a bas-relief of spectators
lifting from the surface but always frozen
halfway through their faces,
        a suggestion of engagement.

And though their identities are varied—
as is often the case with players in a dream—
        the gray paper topiary
of their expressions captures
one common mood: powerlessness.

The puppets are 3D and dance,
as puppets do, on strings
lifted and dropped by invisible hands.
        The puppets, too, are paper mâché
and are still wet where limbs connect.
As one puppet recovers from a stumble,
another is being jerked from its bed.

Bullets whine and slice through the air,
paper puppet mouths open in screams.
  This is a stage of war.
On a nearby stage a few surviving children
pick through a refuse dump;
the sun is hot, pale, indifferent.

Members of the paper mâché audience are demanding
retribution, ransom, access to files.
  Members of the audience remember history.
They hold up thousand-year-old scrolls,
treaties, grocery receipts.
The audience demands change;
the audience is taking bets.

The audience is ineffectual, busy elsewhere.
  War is big business, like any entertainment.
They choose sides, justify regret, send money
to the puppets who fall the best.

The audience pulls up another page,
mixes another drink. They're bored
and want to go home, but
can't find their keys.
  The audience is frozen in a dream.

SUFFRAGE

They pull up the fence posts
for firewood, let the hogs run wild,
use up all our water
to cool the canons,
to rinse the surgeons' hands.

They say the American Civil War
is full of color: the blue coats
of the Yanks, the gray of the Rebels,
    bright red waving in both flags.
Red when the canons overheat, red
soaking into the ground, red
screaming through my dreams—
but always dark when they're done.

This morning it's our turn to bury the dead.
I'm searching for my husband,
for my brothers, for my sister's boy.
I roll 'em over
whether they're breathing or not.
    Either way, I've got to know.

Yesterday, General took all the troops,

the able bodied and the barely moving,
and chased the enemy over the river;
now, it's just us camp followers left.
It'll be a mighty shallow grave we dig
for the other side (God bless 'em).
'Course, we'll make markers for our own.

Across the slopping field
and down in the trampled corn
the stink is starting to rise,
the crows and the vultures and the hogs
    already starting in on the carnage.
If we don't get 'em in the ground
fever will spread to the towns,
poison what's left of the living.

The ones that ain't had nothing
to eat in a week, they turn pale, go white.
The ones that had a little something
in their bellies blow up like a storm—
all puffy and blue and black.
    I'm so afraid
    I won't recognize them.

Listen, there's a sure way to tell
if a man's not going to make it
when he gets shot in the gut:

if he bleeds heart red, doctor him;
if it's mixed with green bile, just hold his hand.
These are the colors of the Civil War.

I hear of the men that lay out there
crippled between the lines,
an orange brush fire set by canon spark
roaring down on them;
    and those same wounded men raising up their heads
for their buddies to see, crying out,
begging to be shot between the eyes.
    The gold of wings
is the only color they care to see.

On the battle field this morning
shoeless medics carry stretched out bodies
in solemn teams of two—
some going to a nearby farm house,
some already flown home.
I raise up from looking into faces,
    think I hear a familiar voice.
It's that same voice I always hear.

They tell me in the future
we'll be better equipped for war.
    Well... you tell 'em this for me:

If ever I could vote,
I would never vote for no person
that's got a mind for war.

JUST IMAGINE INDEPENDENCE DAY

The animated conversation I was overhearing
was of two men in their mid thirties,
one instructive and enthusiastic, the other
wide-eyed and wolfing it down.
I say *enthusiastic* but think about
retracting the word since it implies
being *en theos*, with God.

It was the Fourth of July;
burned spots
in the grass and on the pavement
from last night's Roman Candles,
more advanced pyrotechnics tonight.

We've come a long way
from Black Cats and Lady Fingers;
and that's pretty much what these men
were excited about: weapons and technology.
Every other sentence they were destroying villages.

They used the term, "Making a kill,"
so there was no reference to army recruits,
hospital workers, mechanics, pets, babies,

someone in a cab on their way to a wedding—
just "a kill." Besides,
it was a video game they were describing.

It was happening on a high definition screen
in an office or family room, and now
in the minds of captive listeners at a coffee shop.
Maybe if there was a station break
or even a text feed at the bottom that read:
    This Ad Paid For by Corporations
    Manipulating Your Fear for Money.

But the killing went on—
the rocket's red glare, the bombs
bursting in air (you know the jingle),
entire populations disappeared—remotely.

We can imagine these men
twenty years ago in their bedrooms
playing simulated war games;
headphones and joy sticks,
blurry-eyed with a box of bad pizza.
Their parents in the living room;
ten o'clock news and remote control,
blurry-eyed with a box of bad pizza.

But the story can't end here...

We must imagine them growing up,
imagine them pulling off the headphones,
ending the game, standing up,
walking out of their parents house
into a world where, indeed,
they must fight for their independence,
refuse the program.

Steel Valley Veterans

A locomotive huffs and digs,
pulls on the rails, chews
at the slow gray curve
between blown out glass, empty mills,
hobo hideouts. Above the river
narrow houses, tight enough
to toss a book between,
breath shallow like old men:
    brittle, determined, smelling
of cockroaches, soup, detergent;
thumping with children.
Everyone's waiting for Christmas,
a furlough, or a legal dose.

Listen to your hometown:
the concussive Ka-Clang
of a switch engine dropping off empties,
gust of wind down the tracks,
    clothespins that once belonged
to your mother rusting on the line.
The noon whistle divides
the things that need doing from
those that probably won't get done.

It's hard to remember a time
without war.

It's always the boys, and now the girls,
from our neighborhood that go.
Somewhere suits start new wars
before the last one's finished.
Business that's never done.
Babies go away; some return.
      They come back twitchy;
they come back glazed.
They come back with reasons
that don't make sense,
      yelling like drunken brakemen,
mumbling in beer, looking for Crack.
Or they come back mute.

Their missing arms are outstretched;
their hearts fill the relentless sky.
They stagger into your house,
      spooky, intense.
They are neighbors. They are Americans.
You offer them a kitchen chair,
      a beer, breakfast at 2:AM.
You avoid certain questions, try to connect
events, rebuild synapse. They leave
a graffitied boxcar in your living room.

You have to crawl under it,
over cold rails, to get to the bathroom.
Rust, grease, weeping steel—
    one wheel is too much
for two men alone to budge.

Below the hill, three more
are coming home:
Ka-Clang—kunhk, kunhk, kunhk.

Like Moon

Because they speak a different language;
because they leave their shoes at the door;
because prayer is the compass of their day,
I already had too many ideas about them.

A child's name is his or her first gift in the world.
Choose a name, the prophets say,
that has a pleasant and beautiful meaning.
For boys, names like *Abdullah* or *Abdur Rahman*.
For girls, *Aaila*: beautiful, like moon; or
     Raida: guide, leader, pioneer. I admit,
I don't know the names of those neighbors.

I see their bicycle chained to the downspout;
worn out tire on its way to the dumpster;
reminders from the manager (just like on my door);
the tell tale evidence of children.
Their shoes come and go like signs that say:
     We are at home, cooking,
sleeping, looking up friends on the Internet;
We are not at home, perhaps
at the pool, at a baby shower,
looking for an attorney. Maybe

we are watching the news, nervously,
wondering about that tall, bearded neighbor.
    That's why I smile at them in the parking lot.
It's universal. A smile is a name
that means many things, but when delivered
from the heart, one thing is sure.

I'm a *Stewart* on my mother's side,
a *MacGregor* on my father's.
From her family: a guardian, keeper
of the house, royalty, s sort of custodian.
The name, *Stewart,* is not so popular now
with leaders misusing power, dividing to conquer.
So every day I get to ask:
    What is it to be a gentleman,
the Jack of Hearts, a man of "complete virture,"
    as Kung Fu Tzu would say?

MacGregor is a son of the watchful shepherd.
And we had a lot to watch out for (then and now);
our lands and culture were also stolen.
We, too, came to this America.

And I know the feeling of a king
raising the sword of discernment
to insure everyone's freedom;
    the watchful eye and vigilant heart

of a shepherd sounding the alarm.

On the sidewalk below
I hear the children who are *Afra:*
 reddish brown color of desert, of earth.
They play games with leaves and chalk;
they do the work of growing up;
they face some direction when they pray.
 Their tongues make sounds like water
being dipped from the well,
sounds of a busy kitchen, of many hands
 pulling a net from the sea.
Foreign but familiar, I recognize
the sounds of yearning, of caring parents,
of spontaneous laughter rising, *Aaila,* like moon
from these soon-to-be Americans.

The Locket

The Maw that is the endless mouth
of the North began with corn,
a few ears at a time, then
forests for fuel, animal herds
whose names we will never know,
mountains of sugar, of silver,
hearts of lettuce, sale of dreams.

The Pope gives one continent
to Portugal, one to Spain.
All is extraction, industry.
Produce one thing well, they say,
and purchase the rest from us;
    mono culture, mono God,
mothers in the street.

She holds it close, the locket
with its tiny photos, rose petals,
centimeter of family land. It lays
    upon her breast as stars lay
upon the hills of her hometown,
a town that is still warm,
still, but endangered.

The searchlight of extraction
sweeps the town for a reason
to remove her memories.
She holds the locket, oh so close.
    For her children
she risks the river,
the electric fence that wants her
to dream herself a criminal, become
their debtor, always enslaved.

Darkness-without-soul incarnates
in greedy bodies, the only place
it can inhabit—hard master
of distraction, keeper of the fence.
But there is a bloom upon the heart,
    a flower and a stinger
in the pit of each empty stomach.

A moon rises red and she can't ignore it—
red of her burning town,
    moon of the unwavering harvest.
She may fall, fall hard
in the street, but the locket,
already on its way, goes
from one child's hand to another.

Central Avenue, Our Tattoo

I walk in early morning light past newsstands,
bicycle racks, a couple of suits
sharing folders, skyspace layered with exhaust,
shop doors opening hungry and aimless.
I'm looking for the last door—
it's hard to take any of this seriously.

Backlit Pampas Grass stirs in waves
on the esplanade with each passing bus,
east-facing walls catch light,
hash browns and coffee float
above the street, a musician at 7:am,
flute case open on the sidewalk.
Our interior life must also be reckoned.

Seekers speak of old souls,
cities and traditions rise and die
while sun worshipers smoke by the pool
and stories remake themselves unchecked
in the likeness of the agency.
Anyone believing themselves not homeless here
hasn't begun the walk.

Mountain Laurels share sky with half moon,
Bird of Paradise, Tree of Heaven,
intoxication of Spanish Broom,
but traffic doesn't notice.
Following skirts and falling in love
is not dissimilar to the way I feel
about infinite varieties of vegetation,
their voices louder now, speaking to me.

Summer insects come to the call,
bedrolls up against church doors,
people searching for shade, shelter
from ear-collapsing boom, privacy invasion—
these too may be God's vehicles
furthering the human virus.

Street corners in time lapse
show the movements of ants;
in slower motion I dilate at your passing,
make my first words crawling toward smiles.
And bird song—everywhere!
Small chirps break through walls of brick,
sail under the zip of wires
and above the so-called progress
that's trying to leave without them.

Students stretch power cords,

plug in deep but always monitored,
get married across the line.
He swings the baby over his head,
wakens dreams not yet dreamed;
she laptops to the other side,
speaks Mandarin to a midnight time zone.
If it's connection you want
don't waste your time in print.

If I was sixteen I'd pierce everything,
amputation a possible future thrill, some parts
becoming unnecessary after we finish
eating the insides out of this earth,
break through that sky blue shell.
But for now this street is our tattoo,
and although it appears
that I come and go, I'll be with you
on Central Ave until the sun fades away.

INHERITORS
ode to the Millenniums

They've got moves, this generation
    of half-techs; mudras
    that flash before their faces like a fan.
They've got language
    deep in the dot, volumes that slip
    between three and three and a half.

They've got space to run
    and time running out;
    they've got ear buds, attitudes, online survival.
They've got 24 hours
    to complete this course, a cab ride,
    three transfers, utilities to tap.

They've got a house to tear down,
    a highway to hit,
    miles and miles and bad wire.
They've gotta be kidding,
    but they're not looking back,
    and that's why they're going to make it.

They've got signals coming at them

expanding synapse, room
for everything; dream levels 1 through 4.
They've got Samurai deletion,
threads to follow, a framework
collapsing and expanding on the fly.

They've got meeting places
that accommodate millions but last
for only a minute, poverty to manage, multiplicity.
They've got food we've never seen,
computers that bleed;
their hearts lie beyond the body.

Hunting Down Death

LUCKY

They said it was destiny
that gave Lucky distemper,
his runny eyes, crusty nose, shivering
in the laundry room out back.
It wasn't a boy's idea
of a dog, that's for sure.
I dreamed tongue-flapping joy
loping beside me,
an after school friend.
It seemed cruel: that invisible hand
    that weakened him
and locked him in the shed.

All winter it was just him and Jessie;
the thump, slide and hiss of her iron
hour after hour—pressed percale,
white linens and stiff shirts for upstairs.

I felt guilty for not going more often.
I heard the urgent whimpers
building to yelps, being eased
    by Jessie's chocolate voice,
strong and calm

like that wide brown river
that ran through our town;
her sure thick arms
reaching into the hot washer.

Hazels' man never came inside.
He'd finish with the yard
    and wait at the end of the drive
in whatever old car they drove that week
while she patted dough
into evening dumplings,
me at the kitchen counter
mesmerized by every move.

One day Hazel,
after talking with Jessie,
stepped into the yard
wiping batter on her apron,
a fat black hand levered on her hip
    and commanded,
"You need to clean up your dog's mess!"
I felt scared.
I didn't really think she'd
lose her job, but gosh,
that was awful uppity talk.

If I'd have thought

it was okay to speak out myself
I would have said,
Lucky, get up, damn it.
But something in him was already
     struggling to be in this world,
disjointed and wobbly as he was,
and no doubt, Hazel's chicken grease
is what pulled him through—
it helped keep me on track.

There were outbreaks of summer storms
across the South that year—
the early '60s and weather was rough,
creeks flooding, bodies
floating down the rivers.
     I couldn't see it, but I could feel it.
Hazel and Jessie never said a word.

By Daffodil time Lucky and I were
in the yard putting anything between us
that would bring a growl,
make him stronger.
But distemper left its mark.
     Like a chain wrapped tight
around the base of a young tree,
Lucky's front legs never grew
an inch past puppyhood.

"Rail Job," my friends teased,
because he looked like a formula dragster,
a raked front end
with tiny wheels in front
and monsters on the rear,
revving on the line,
    waiting for the light to change.
Those fronts had to spin
twice as fast to keep up—and they did!
He was coming from behind.

That year Lucky's yelp became a bark
beside my bicycle;
Jessie hauled her bundles
back and forth to the house;
Hazel nodded from her dishes
at the kitchen window
and that brown river got stronger and wider
with each coming storm.

LA BACA

I got good at playing cards, at gambling. In Tulsa County Jail there's little else, just that same old "somebody done me wrong song," the clang of bolted doors, cackling hyena laughs and brass keys raking the bars. In the morning I collected two or three trays of soggy toast and sweet white rice, my winnings from the night before. Those guys with cash would be bailing out in a few days anyway, too nervous to eat, trying to remember where they threw the gun, some bitch talking to the D.A.

One easy touch was The Baca. He had a face like a cow. Cholo gang member's would walk by, snap him on the head and sing "La Ba-ca," two octaves above Middle C. I could see that shooting Valo and huffin' glue had wiped out half his western states and the railroads connecting them. But he was gentle and didn't mean any harm so I'd talk to him. Besides, we were the same age—seventeen.

I pulled chains in January, that is: I went on down to McAlester, to the Big House. It was embarrassing when he said, "Good-bye, see you later." I thought, *Man, you don't say that shit; your moma ain't here and characters come and go!* Actually, that was more out of some movie; all I said was, "see ya." I felt strangely protective but that could be dangerous; associations had to be loose. It's like war—no, it *is* war—at the beginning and at the end you got to be able to shift, to flow, to let go and move on when new boundaries are drawn. Light on your feet—know what I mean?

I didn't arrive at Granite until sometime in May. I had a delay back at the Big House—four months on The Rock, shaved heads, one Pall Mall a week with a 30.30 watching from the rail. A bunch of guys started a riot and my cell was one of the first ten to go. *It was nothin' but a thing.* But by the time I hit Receiving I'd put my feelings on lockdown. Fifteen years later an alcoholism counselor helped me identify my first emotional state—terror.

Up and down the run you could hear the primal rhythm of defense, the schh-schh, schh-schh of issue toothbrushes being sharpened on concrete to an eye-poking point, the new regiment preparing for war. When I looked up from my tool making there was The Cow.

"Sure," I said, cause he seemed to already know the ropes and was the only face I recognized. So when I hit population I moved into his cell on one of the white runs, first floor. We talked about our hometown on the other side of the state, what we remembered of parties, movies, girls; we talked about staying alive in the joint. In and out of being confused he was earnest—I could see that. But after a few days I put in for a transfer and hoped he'd make it.

It got real simple, The Cow had love letters and cigarettes arriving every day—propositions—and they weren't coming from home. It was a matter of time before they'd make him a punk and I had to turn the other way. Associations are everything in a pressure tank—you belong here, or you belong there. I didn't have the language for those kinds of good-byes, but I was learning fast what to say and what not to say. "Sorry, Baca," was all I could say then, though I'd certainly say more now if I got the chance.

Later that year I'd see La Baca on Saturdays out in the yard with a few other guys bunched up against the fence. He never showed any resentment for me moving on, for surviving, just those soulful brown eyes gazing across the cotton fields, waiting, always waiting for somebody to open the gate.

Getting The News

I was passed out in the back of Larry's panel delivery truck, a '49 Chevy, primer gray, with the word "FISH" in block letters two feet high on both sides. The handle racked, the back doors cracked and God's light broke in like a handgun across the first morning. They found me hung over, tangled in a blanket, curled around oil cans, a jack handle, some band equipment. It was January.

My friends hauled me out and over to my mom's place on the south side. All my hippie and outlaw buddies looked out of place sitting on that Victorian furniture but strangely, like an empty glass finally filled, the house now had some awkward purpose, not just life sized knickknacks arranged on high-pile carpet.

Theopholis Smith was there, too, the first black man I could remember to enter through the front door of her house. Theo ran a drug program down in town. Years before he had waken in the morgue of some eastern city with a tag on his toe—so the story went.

He was saying something about how my brother's passing would create an opportunity for me and my mom to get closer, but I was having a hard time looking at her. I could feel her staggering through the currents of her Vodka and Valium and that overwhelming pain that I'd always been so afraid of.

Her hysteria hung like flammable gas, like cigar smoke in a back bedroom where her sanity was brokered night after night, a Hitchcock kind of reality. The guys were looking at me like I was hanging on the end of a long thin rope from the top of a twenty story building. No one came right out and said the word *suicide*, but they said he lived for a few hours with a bullet in his brain, long enough for her to wail over his body in a coma.

Communication as I learned it was a series of postures: slamming doors; heavy sighs; drunk gushy, "Come here's"; a father disowning his oldest son; a language of loaded guns and withdrawals of love. There's a lot of ways to say, "I'm hurting," a lot of ways to say, "Fuck you," and it was going to take a long time to sort through this without my older brother, someone on the inside to take some of the blame, show me the way out.

After the boys all left I sat there with the drapes drawn trying to imagine what a good person would do, what my dad would do. Then I remembered—it was my dad's birthday—and this must have been my brother's patiently planned wish.

This Dog Won't Hunt

"Come on, take a ride," he said,
I've got some business
out to the house."
Everybody knew Floyd
and Yvonne were breaking up,
camps divided, blame laid,
folks pushing away from tables
shaking their heads.

Late summer in the Cookson Hills
back roads were choked
with Polk, wild Hemp, Sumac.
Floyd wrestled the wheel
    to stay out of the ruts.
A lariat of dust spiraled at my feet
among burrito wrappers, beer cans.
I thought to run my finger
along the dash, plow
a furrow of that Oklahoma dirt,
but how a man keeps his truck
    is his business
and I didn't want
to appear sissy, so I didn't.

Floyd's mind was steady,
    somewheres else.

We pulled up in the yard
next to a horse trailer with a flat,
bed frame stacked up,
Styrofoam cooler full of car parts.
I jumped out, didn't think to ask,
just stood there flapping my sweaty shirt
    while Floyd pulled a rifle
from behind the seat.
I followed him around back.

They wiggled and yelped
when he came up,
tails like water snakes
whipping the air, throwing
their bodies against chain link.
There were two hunting dogs
in one pen and three more
in cages of their own.
We stood there
silent for a while
    in the buzz of katydids,
all that eager saliva.

"I just don't know," Floyd said,

"how I'd take care of 'em now—
I'll see you back at the truck."

CATALPA WALTZ

Saturday afternoon in town,
you and me for groceries, the kids
dangling on the end of summer strings,
towering Catalpa trees in bloom,
    crawdads quick and blue,
some thunder rolling in the hills—
we might have said we were in a hurry,
but we had no idea what it meant back then.

Suddenly the screen door on the store
banged out, a pair of blue jays squawked,
an asphalt-buckling elm lifted a brow
and somebody yelled, "Chicken."

Sure enough, neck stretched low
and taking brief positions under hot pickups,
    a game hen was on the loose
amid amused bystanders, traffic on pause.
We'd all but given up when the practiced hand
of a hard-shoed grandma held up the prize
    and asked the kids, "you wont it?"

We were there in the '53 Chevy

drove down from Canada—
a wide and wonderful place with names
like Kalamalka and Kamloops;
just as strange as these local tongue twisters:
Tahlequah and Tsalagi.

So we put that bird in the back with the boys
    and named her Dixie, though we knew
that during the war in Oklahoma
the Cherokee fought on both sides of the line.

Water begets water, life gravitates
toward the center then explodes
and chickens don't stay single.
We wedged orchard crates in notches of trees
just low enough to reach in and surprise the eye
with a soft new color, occasional crazy shape.

In the Cookson Hills everything gets shared
with the coons—minnows, eggs, tomatoes.
And if you're not paying attention
someone might harvest your smoking materials,
kitchen gardens the logical place
to grow herbs and remedies.

But we had plenty of everything,
lived on nearly nothing, listened to frogs

and the plip-plop-plop song of water
falling through leaves wide as a pond,
   that Catalpa Waltz played steady
by long sweet summer rains.

The Hard Time
for the woman standing next to me in the San Jacinto County Jail

See how the cops file in,
pointing, circling you with accusations,
their flat feet set far apart.
See how they line up,
not knowing what they're saying,
secretly seeking your forgiveness,
not believing in themselves nor
anything else, just locker room talk.

And you will endure even this.

And those for whom you have no pity,
pass them over; the devil you see in them
is not worth your attention.
But for those whom you see
in their fear and pitiful arrogance,
and feel even one leaf
of falling sorrow, turn
toward your heart and nod—
this one deserves better.

In a moment they'll call you

into a separate room, handcuffed
you'll stumble
through questions of their choosing,
handcuffed you'll attempt
to deflect their blame with indifference,
but inevitably your pain will betray you.

And you will endure even this.

Later when you're alone and the clang
of iron and humiliating laughter
die into night's hollow cell,
take that time for yourself—
that's the hard time!

That's the bullet that ricochets in the brain,
the edge of knowing and hate
blurred on the same blade,
your own ragged procession
lining up for your forgiveness.

They'll throw themselves before you:
that child unworthy of rescue;
the girl who couldn't say "Help;"
the woman who tells herself
she's not smart enough to see it coming;
the teenager who swore

it would never happen again;
the woman last night
who was finally big enough
to wield a razor.

And you will endure even this.

Rapport

The speed of sound is 770 mph. The speed of a bullet
can vary from just under that to over 3,000 mph.

His blog reminded me about the speed
of bullets. How, at a distance,
you hear the whizzy whine
of projected lead, then
    the decision of the gun, the rapport.
I've been shot at twice.

Both times it was because I won,
    but you can't say I wasn't warned.
Florida Highway A-1-A is sketchy,
a wayward hem running on and off
the cloth of the Atlantic Coast.
We stopped in for a beer, the rack
and crack of pool balls across green felt.

Let him win, said Dave, he's crazy
and he's got a piece in his pocket.
Most of the time I lose but not because I want to.
"Fuck him... eight in the side."
    And then we ran and ran,
rapport,   rapport, rapport!

Whizzy whine all around us.

A salt dome of pink granite rises
hundreds of feet, windblown and crumbling,
off the valley floor where the Goshute Tribe
leases land to the Feds, buries toxic waste.
She told me he would shoot us.

No one knew for sure what went on
in Jeff's mind—just hallways,
dark hallways and sinkholes to hell.
Everyone that got close
    was liable, liable to slip.
An hour to Salt Lake, a missile range
to the west, Jeff with a rifle in the rocks—
Skull Valley was well-named.
He told us later, he wasn't really
    aiming to kill us,
and the sheriff believed him.
Jeff was slick.

At that distance we heard
spinning lead first, confirmed
by pops like firecrackers under a can
coming from the rocks.
Zing—pop,   zing—pop.

But Jeff was right. I had no business
    climbing unstable debris.
Sometimes it's best
to let the other guy clean the table.

Dodge City, then West

We pulled over every hundred miles
to dump canteen water
on each others' heads. It was summer
from Oklahoma through Kansas
to Colorado, my first trip
to the Rocky Mountains with my father.
4-60 air-conditioning—
all four windows down, occasional grasshopper.

High Plains elevation lifted like a drain board
across America's heartland,
shimmered Emerald City promise.
We paralleled the rails,
    kept an eye out for speed traps,
the budding fins of the '56 Fleetwood
catching our drift.

"Boot Hill, take a look, son."
But it was dad's stories
that brought the prairies to life:
the half finger he'd left
in a West Texas oil field, accounts
of Pretty Boy Floyd that blurred

with his own boyhood just after statehood.
Heck, the ol' man was 22 by the time Wyatt Earp died.

    Cornfields, Meadow Larks, cornfields.
    Prairie Dogs, Antelope, wind.

Dad's Old Crow bottle rolled from under the seat
when farmers pulled out in front of us,
Arkansas wine and rifles shifting in the trunk.
I didn't care
for cornball and roadside curios;
quickly bored with historic markers,
I wanted the cops on our tail.

I wanted to grab the shaft of that arrow,
pull the chert point from my breast,
    stand up and spit on the ground.
I wanted to hold that long-skirted woman
around her schoolmarm waist;
look a mountain lion in the eye.

I wanted to stand at the holy altar
of Bierstadt's canyons,
negotiate passage with Catlin's chiefs,
    pan for my own God damned gold;
and a week later in Manitou Springs I did,
with a hubcap off the Cadillac. Thanks, dad.

On the road you're always young or old enough,
but looking back my work wasn't
in the things I did. My deeds
don't have wings in this world—
I'm here to witness.

At another time, around another fire
I'll make my report—I doubt this is it.

Just the same, my name is Meriwether Lewis;
my name is Sacajawea; my name
is Negro Henry Hilton.
My name is the silent sound of a red tail
    dropping like a rock
on the rabbit of so-called civilization.

My name sits up in a shallow grave,
steals a horse, rides out of Dodge.
My name is the untameable forward motion
of a bullet, a flash flood, a falling star,
a man hunting down Death—
and not in some casual way.

I see your wild rivers limping
on their way to the ocean;
purple mountains sold off
in sections of majesty,

the branded image of liberty rolling
like a wheel cover into the ditch.
     But that's not Death.
That's just life doing its best.

Glass insulators sparkled on faded crosses
as the sun sang its "You're Mine, All Mine" song.
The blacktop rolled out ahead of us;
the Santa Fe Trail turned south;
the prairie grass got shorter and shorter.

The Atchison and Topeka was put down
fifteen miles a day on the flats;
we stayed ahead of schedule
since we weren't laying any track.
I asked my dad how fast we'd have to go
to keep the sun from setting.
     He gave me degrees and lines of longitude,
     let me do the math;
and that day the earth became *round*—
I never again had to take that for granted.

The difference between school and learning
also came into view.
You've got to *walk* the curve of this earth,
tilt with the seasons, mark moonrise
year after year with a rock,

love like it's all in vain, die
little by little and call it growing up.
You've got to pull over at Garden City
and freeze your parts in the middle of summer
in that giant artesian pool.

I was riding shotgun and it's a good thing
we were the only highwaymen on the road
crossing the Kiowa Grasslands because,
as usual, I was lost in a daydream.
Dad was in the crow's-nest, spied them first,
quietly called out, "Mountains."

The kiss is never the dream, and the dream
can never be the mountain. At first
a disappointment, "Are those the Mighty Rockies?"
    Then it comes to you... and it comes to you,
an apparition drawing near, improbable topography,
enchanted world pale and beckoning
beyond the known, a trick of perception.
By wagon, a few days—by car, maybe two hours,
distance as an idea twisting like a spoon.

At first that jagged procession
rose and fell with dips in the road,
came and went in the waves of August;
later, it became the province of my life,

bride of the desert, holy illusion
from which I've had little desire to escape.
Every view was my gosh-darn-first; now
    I hold every sunset as my last.

A couple of weeks later we turned around,
took the southern route back;
that is to say, Oklahoma by way of New Mexico.
    Raton Pass—whoo hoo—and you're up and over
where the land is constantly made anew. From it
mountains grow, trees and grasses,
dark and light skinned peoples, birds blue and yellow.
You can feel the plates sliding on the waves,
stars blooming on the horizon.

My dad is long gone now, and the moon
has touched that farthest rock six times.
I've already said goodbye to Dodge,
    paid my respects,
now I'm saying hello
to that trail that's only meant for the wind.
I'm taking one last look
    and I'm calling it... good.

Time To Think

Because we were sitting in the Route 66 Diner
having milk shakes and sweet things
with cherries on top; and because
our dates were still flushed from two hours
of dancing Salsa; and because Buddy Holly
was swinging and singing about
the door to his heart; and because
it had been almost forty years
since I had to fight for my life,
I wasn't ready with a response when you said
they should execute second offenders.

Most of the time I can find something to agree with,
some point of view to get behind.
I can talk about oil and trees
and energy without uttering "green;"
discuss common decency and never
involve Dr. King, Confucius or Jesus. I can lean
into conversations, ride the waves of Grace
and never even use that word.
But that night I wasn't prepared
for injection, electrocution or a firing squad.

And because I know that you were law enforcement
in the Midwest and saw horrendous acts;
and because I can guess at your own childhood,
at situations that made it easier to identify
with the perpetrator rather than admit powerlessness;
and because you teach 4th and 5th graders
in the South Valley and I would need more time
to develop your curriculum plan,
all I could think to say was that execution
was the easy way out for criminals,
and didn't give them time to think, time to feel.

And because I had been set up at seventeen
by my brother with an eighth of an ounce of pot,
but never the less did hard time, and four years later
got caught smoking a joint with a nurse who could afford
an attorney and so I ended up doing another stint;
and because although I think I've paid my dues
I always wonder how I can contribute more to life;
and because at that moment I found myself
on the verge of tears which caught me off guard,
and we were in such a good wholesome place
with the girls and the banana splits,
the kind of places I dreamed about in the slammer,
I couldn't look you in the eye and say,
"If you'd gotten your way
I wouldn't be here tonight."

Yay Yay, Because I Couldn't Say Yellow

I don't remember crying into my rabbit
or if I talked to it at all,
but I held it around the neck
until its floppy-eared head
fell to the side, until our DNA
were the same.

Sometimes I'd pull my thumb
out of my mouth and
speak to people, but not often.
Funny how stuffed toys will be
genderless if you let them,
how they know and know and know,
their words also few.

Yay Yay, like most special friends that lived
with the children in our neighborhood,
knew the ways of the garden: azaleas,
rollie-pollies, the silence of snow;
knew the smell of boiling water
just before rolled oats
were poured into pot; the sound
of parents fighting in the next room;

the signal from other helpers
coming and going through my dreams.

And I don't remember saying goodbye
when finally I stood up on the tricycle,
one foot on the platform between the rear wheels,
one foot paddling the sidewalk,
both hands gripping the bars,
and headed off to science experiments
with fireworks, girls, jail, Oregon,
wild rivers, the Internet.

Yay Yay is not the invisible friend
I've spoken of, not the teacher
or even the Jack of Hearts, but last night
after another heart attack
I reached across the pillow absentmindedly,
my fingers searching for the feel
of threadbare, yellow terry cloth.

I Say, Let Them Live

SHE'S KIN

I woke up dead in a wax museum,
reached for our playhouse and porch swing,
for daddy's gun, for a bucket
to pull up the rest of the dream.
I reached for you, sister,
but the furniture had changed.
Apparently this was not the life
I took to sleep last night,
     not the now it once was.

     When the tall grass gave way
     to the short grass
     and the scattered line of wagons
     creaked and howled for grease,
     the men kicked Mama's piano
     off into the dust. You and me
     not big enough yet to run alongside.
     Back in St. Louis folks imagined it
     full of arrows, a last b-flat
     ending the hymn of her hope.
     From then on she was a *pioneer woman*—
     and don't you forget it.

I've always wondered why it's been

to water that I'm drawn,
kissing women by the well, taking them
down by the river, ripping their skirts
until it rains. I chase storms and joy.
Every woman is you, and none.

      By the time Mama made California
      there was nothing left
      of the promise. Too much gold,
      frost bite, cannibalism.
      When the wind blows smoke from the coast
      you can see her facing the breakers
      where she held us both
      beneath the waves, out with the tide.
      Mama just standing there—
      her wet feet, her cooking sherry,
      her Lydia Pinkham's,
      finally, the paregoric.

When I heard your songs on stage
I said, She's kin.
Got to be.
Who else could sing with the sea
in her voice, make sense
of a double drowning?

I Hear Joy on My 60th Birthday
The Duende Poetry Series, Placitas, NM - 2010

She arrives with many colors, horizons,
a small band of warriors,
morning glories to the tips of her fingers.
Her horses also come, arriving before her,
running loose on the road, telling jokes
in the meadow, plotting against us.
They arrive hot and sweaty,
full of jazz notes; the children inside them
     visible when they gallop across the sun.
We're cousins but could have married.

And though we've written ourselves
a thousand times into the future
some flood of pride or ragging battalion
has always shaped itself between us.
Damn those brass buttons!

When I was younger I smelled her horses
racing the waves, prancing
     before water without end.
I chased them west into the storm of my life,
left her singing in a plum grove.

Of all the foolish things.

But I've done worse—
walked like a zombie on the face
of the mother, thought myself separate;
reached for hawks, lost my footing;
made my solitary camp in the hills above the village.
    Sometimes her horses ran with mine.

At night they wander the highways,
a hazard in headlights;
at dawn, a silhouette for sunrise;
at noon, caught again, always a few missing.
Today, finally, everything is enough;
    nothing fully satisfied.
I have seen her.

I've seen her crawling backwards
over her own knives of stubbornness,
sleeping with a lost tribe,
sheltering dogs.
    Trust her
when she speaks of enemies.
Take the reed in your teeth.

She spreads her blessing
as a blanket beneath the council tree,

a bed of bright lights at the bottom of the lake.
   Mud, blue birds, corn pollen.
   Know our galaxy in the depths of her gaze.

Because of her my heart is closer,
but I'm not here to get in her way.
She ignores me and it's best
   for both of us, besides,
I have horses of my own.

Boondockin' at Jemez Springs

If you bring your own bullets
to Los Ojos Bar you can pull
one of twenty guns off the wall,
settle an argument, start a revolution,
step into the road and celebrate
the sound of your own longing
disappearing up canyon. You can
    run your fingers along
the curve of the past;
rub the patina of instant friendship,
old memories, lip-to-ear whispers,
    interlocking-thigh talk.
You can wedge matchbooks
and paper napkins under table legs
but it's not going to last.

Later, you'll write songs
about the boys who just wanted
    one thing, but that night
everybody's passport was good
and the band kept playing country ways.

A mountain man comes into town;

wood smoke and books under rock ledges.
Maybe he just wants one thing,
one thing at a time that is—
he dances wild in front of the fire,
he talks crazy-talk on the table,
    he takes the girls outside,
shows them how many stars.
He heads back up the hill by himself.

All this goes down
while cowpokes scramble to partner up.
You duck into the little girl's room
for a last swipe of lipstick.
When the bar lets out the cops
are long gone. Nobody wants the call.
    If some drunk starts a fire tonight,
we'll have work for weeks in the forest.
But don't kid yourself,
even stars on the desert are fragile.

Sleeping for Someone Else's Dream

The smell of concrete finishing in forms,
strike of morning sun on rebar,
lunch pails fat in the truck.
Somebody hollers, "laminate it,"
and a pew of hammers falls in,
slapping board to board, echo to bang;
    neighborhoods from nothing,
vacant lots disappearing like prairies.
I tried to grow up here.

When I was eight years old
I was Captain Midnight
with an airbase in Argentina
and a Canary Yellow XKE convertible.
All the girls were wild about me
    and there was that one
who fell for me over and over
not knowing that I could fly.
But I was a good and simple hero
beneath all that irresistibility and science,
despite the fact that I was going to save the world;
despite the fact that I was too shy to even speak.

And I was brave then—
though I never thought so—
battling Scarlet Fever
    and other attempts on my life.
It was for my parents that I fought those battles,
for their frontier family hopes,
their claim to these pastures of plenty.
I really wasn't up to it,

but their hearts were already so broken
and I had their eyes and their English hands
and this timber across my back.
    I was crossed at birth by a two-headed doctor.
I could never find a way to tell them that.

I was as bewildered as they by all of this,
but I jumped in the hole never the less,
set pumps against the flood,
swung hammers for America,
gnawed on my end of the chain.
    I had to create my own dream worth living.

And the dream morphed—
it had the face of a migrant mechanic,
the feet of a factory, the voice
of a soldier a long way from home.
The dream changed with landscape,

elevation, how the table was set.
Some days it followed the watercourse,
some days it blew up dams.
Some mornings I lagged too far behind,
    some mornings too far out in front;
but most always I was a whore
to the world in which I lived.

Every backseat and urban tribe
was a momentary shelter, a train station
in the jungle, a four-poster draped in batik,
a thread of drifters to which I became a shiny knot.
    For every shore: an interior needing trails;
    for every river: an ocean in which to die;
    for every summer love:
    the lonesome call of winter.

It takes a long time to wrestle
the mountains of the past, see them
for what they are. It takes a long time
to wade through the choiceless choices.
Go to Yoga or to the shooting range;
    feed the birds or have them for lunch;
take your sex standing up or upside down.
Everything matters—then—it doesn't.

I told myself story after story;

I tried to sell you those stories, too.
   Whose dream this is, is anybody's guess
but I'm beginning to suspect that it's not mine.
I'll claim it, nevertheless... then, return it,

   but I don't recommend following me.
If there's water in the next canyon
you'll know where to turn.

Night Ride with my Make Believe Friend

After dancing—the coffee shop;
after chocolate pie—the highway.

It's just a loop around the city
but I could spin out any direction:
west into the desert in search of
    hard-to-find darkness;
north to meet with my teachers;
east into the mountain
to begin again; south
on my own *Journada del Muerto*.

It's a different girl every week.
Tonight she's a saxophone-playing rock star,

mixed blood, split tongue, heart
    like an arrow.
I do most of the talking.

She's getting to know me
but already knows too much.
She cuts through with questions like:
    "Where's your water, your song;

what do hear from the Ancestors;
what the hell are you doing here, anyway?"
Kind of spirited for an *imaginary* girl,
but by the time we skirt Santa Ana res
we both let down, admit
    that love has changed;
there's no gain in blame,
not even our own;
and there's no going back.

This new love is big
and lonesome and loaded
with sharp-sided cliffs that drop off
into narrow nothing.
    If we stand still
all the animals step into the moonlight,
circle around us, and people
needing a healing find one another—
sometimes when they don't even believe.

Streets in the new neighborhoods
are wide and smooth, a dream glide,
    sometimes a well-lit funeral.
But we're not looking for red dust
and washboard roads tonight—
though it's in our bones as sure as starvation,
misappropriation and genocide.

It's not a crime to remember our past
but find ourselves on a different path, besides,
nobody truly walks by themselves.
Like she says, "Ultimately,
    we are all one."

I drop her off at her make-belief truck
and all she says is, "Thanks,"
which might mean:
    I was needing a break
and somebody who wouldn't try to figure me out.
I nod, let her open her own door.
I'm all talked out.

FRIEND, LOVER, WHATEVER

I push you away, you follow;
I ignore you, you swerve into my lane.
When I court you, you mock me
and spin on your heels.
You are always the other woman.

The whack of your long knife
loves melons; wet quarters
lay open on the block.
Coconuts and severed dreams drift
out to sea. You want me
deep, gnawed down to nothing.

I've quit speculating on other lives.

I walk with you through the village,
my personal blanket loose
about my shoulders—a close friend,
sometimes too close. Last night
I wandered the streets
with no *body* at all.

When you're near me I'm dying

to know more about you,
your red lips, the cool edge of your blade.
When I'm without you
I charge headlong, kicking up rocks,
meaning nothing.
It's you that lifts up my life, you
bringing meaning
to spilled seeds and juice on the board.

SINGING FOR THE SURFACE

If I was drowning and you were with me
riding the gray folds of the sea
we could go down together, sinking
through the sonnets of my life.

There are cities here
and as I lived them they blurred;
the waking cities and the ones of dreams—
a lopsided porch with faded floorboards,
original prayer flags made from dresses,
hippies hanging like monkeys on the rail.

Hans held the baby sweetly
while her mother and I slipped
    deeper into the forest, loving
until the trees quaked. Next morning
we picked pie cherries for pennies;
at night the northern lights, a green wheel
whipping across the Canadian Rockies.

I tried to make two bucks once
at the 59th Street bathrooms on the seawall,
his stubbled face sucking needful

in the front seat as we parked on the beach.
I couldn't get it up—
but I asked for the money anyway
to show the older guys who put me up to it.
Belonging, all of us needed belonging.

A machine shop in Chicago, everything
by the bells; start, stop, pay the man,
     bundle yourself
against that forty-foot razor blade,
but don't teach those immigrants English,
don't be a trouble maker. Fear,
and just that, passed
from one boss to another.

Driving south with my father
toward San Antonio, buying street clothes
to replace my prison dungarees.
     Parole, and even more secrets
between us now. He drove and drove,
so anxious to show me
the wonders of Hemisfair, a world beyond
work gangs in cotton fields;
his love was silent, holding, hopeful—
the blazing Texas sun from hell,
map on the dash of the Buick,
his fedora.

Pounding tables with blue books,
ash trays, coffee cups. By the grace of God,
that was our therapy and confessional.
I looked you in the eye and said,
"I stole everything I could have earned:
attention, respect, a little touch."
Later you said, "It's all unmerited gift."

The softness of a woman's cheek
    was a peach against all wars
and the colorless landscape of progress.
Faces revolving in desire, faces
in stern anguish, in simple acceptance.
Tender faces colliding in waves.
All that closeness and still
a mystery, fleeting whiffs of perfume.
    We can look at one another now;
my witness here will tell you why.

Mr. DeWitt lived at the top of the hill.
I don't see his face,
    only the morning flowers he cut
when I rode my tricycle there,
steering with one chubby arm,
coasting back down the buckled sidewalk
to surprise my sleeping mom.
    My sleeping mom.

We see her trembling
on her knees before the priest,
first woman in a business suit,
asking me to zip up the back of her dress;
thermometer, briefcase, French Toast.
    You never really abandoned me.

If I was drowning, but it was okay,
I could go on like this for days,
the details washing over me
settling like sand and bits of shell;
    more than memories,
poems buoying me up, that bubble
racing for the surface.

THE LAST UMBRELLA
another road poets poem for Synchrodestiny

Drive north at ninety
across the green skirts of short grass,
volcanoes side by side paused
in the molten making of earth.
Here bouquets of white roses billow
above pale mountains, fill their hearts
for a good afternoon cry.
This is one love
    that's constant, certain,
in it for the destruction, laying itself
like a lamp at your feet.
This is one love you can't out drive.

In Denver there are friends.
You must pass as a novitiate
through construction, speed traps,
days of numbing ticky-tack, products,
flight patterns, invisible grids.
You must be determined!

You are a river emptying, emptying,
unaware of what you give.

You are a warrior dying
over and over in the arms of your enemy;
    you are closer than ever.

I'm not coming back, my friend says,
Not doing this one again—
and I know the feeling
though I hold up everything now
as just another story: reincarnation,
the need for salvation, train wreck or
fluttering dove at the end of the tunnel.

I'm piercing the city
in search of an address, a simple
backyard fire, an assembly of misfits
    absentminded about their halos.
I am broken, a piece of broken bread.

A circle of friends is a wreath
above your door—if you're here
    you've already knocked. Come,
sisters and brothers;
you are the forgotten in this world,
the migration and very juice,
the last umbrella.

DECIDED ON TREES

I've decide on trees.
Not at my next funeral—
that's really none of my business;
you do whatever makes *you* feel good—
    but at that moment when I turn,
pen in one hand, stone in the other,
a river to merge.

These are my friends—trees—
our nearest neighbors, first companions
in the new world.
Some would say *rocks are the ancestors*

and that wouldn't be wrong,
    our constitution being the same,
varying only in percentages.
I'd be red, too, with more iron,
yellow with sulfur.
    When I slow down
I see those stones bending
in the breeze, drinking at the shore.

But trees are the ones

I want to usher me through.

I dig on how they sweep the ground,
shout out, raise up and up
like they do; all the while
    hauling buckets to the sky.
They know just the right words,
know just the right fruit
to feed each of their guests—besides,
I like their sense of humor.
I've decide on trees.

I'm gush-struck, kind of giddy
beside them when they hand me
a prism and say, "Look at me this way,"
leaf patterns fanned out in code.
    Each cluster is an epic tale:
frondsy tropical stories,
fringed whispers before the moon;
towering North Americans;
carpets of climbers at alpine elevations;
    and tiny trees with tiny birds
in tiny worlds where chameleons
are lost in bright green play.

On this side we burn—
piles of smoldering leaves

beside the wall, scarred thighs
from running through prairie fires,
faggots crackling at the base of a witch,
    levels of dreaming going up in smoke.
But they've got that all figured out.
I think they've chosen me, too.

On the boulevard today Sycamores
are all whicky-whacky in the wind.
I could jump in, toss with them.
Gee, I don't know how we'll appear
when we come through, or
if it's even a matter of crossing.
I only know I want trees there.

I Have Come to Say This

The idea of dancing up some rain
causes the road's skin to quiver,
perks the ears of otherwise
drowsy mountains.

Maybe these fools will finally feel
the sun shining through their eyes;
maybe we'll go home
on the same horse after all.

The Texans at the next table
are obsessed, obnoxious—
I say, let them live.

It's true they copulate and have children
but we should save our strength
for greater enemies.

A poisoned river runs
through our land *and* theirs—
same water, same need for prayer.

Snow is hiding in the mountain;

the ocean is angry, but
for good reason.

We fed these strangers
when they arrived skinless and blinking,
now, we must teach them to sing.

A Soft Halleluiah

Every Mouth

I walk the body around in circles.
I pace the rooms of this house,
seeing with the thoughts
of my mothers, my fathers, the procession
of oxygen and wheat and wildebeest.

The miracle of just one leaf.

My ancestors—the trees;
my breath rolling with thunder
through the mountain.

If not in all that I see
(and surely not in what I do)
then where, if where is a what
that can be known?

I will sit this body down,
a hunger strike stubborn as a bug.
I have called all the names I know.
No more names!

I have searched, and searching

is a game. If I'm out of time
then postponement is also a lie.

Kindness. Connection. What else?

My voice shouts through every mouth.
These words are not my own.

HAVING NOTHING LEFT TO DO

Let's say they wake you,
about 3:00 AM, and you enter
the conversation with a question
about mortality, about the body.
But let's say they redirect you
and tell you there's nothing left to do.
"Should I visit my birthplace,
write my memoirs?" *Not necessary,*
they say, *Your tasks are complete.*
"What about another book of poetry?"
Only if you want to.

There's a sensation you call joy,
and in the morning you try to bring meaning to it,
the quality, the cause, a description
of the interlocking visuals that accompanied it.

And here's the part that didn't happen:
You tidy up your things, put books and papers
in understandable stacks, wash
the last cup, change the sheets—
all these things out of respect for those
who will find it and have to deal with it—

then you lay it down sweetly and move
to the window of this dream.

It's a bit disorienting—retirement.
At first, of course, immense relief,
but old habits want to pull the trigger
like a severed finger—your lunch pail,
your hard hat, your fear of financial security!
But every morning the world again;
no ticket in the mail.
Now you're grumpy that you're disappointed.
That's no way to feel,
you grump to yourself.

Then, let's say, a woman appears
(this part happening in the world).
Her body warm, her eyes clear pearls
that open into the sea, her thoughts
tables of food, everything edible here.
"Now you're free to do whatever you please,"
she says.   And that sounds true...

something you've never done, perhaps
an exotic trip, a daring exploration,
something you couldn't do before
because of all those distractions, something
you wouldn't let yourself do because and because...

Then it comes—simply—
the only answer, really.   Love.

And though you always said
that you weren't good at it
and didn't really know what it was,
you remember love is that
when all else is exhausted and fails,
and it has nothing to do
with coming or going, never did;
and suddenly it seems doable.

And let's say that you begin,
starting with her, and so you do.

Parasol

The father walking, the child
 on his shoulders,
  a greening summer,
   top of the morning.

A round mouth making la-la,
 yellow umbrella spinning,
  a song matching the going.

Overhanging oaks, insects
 dancing, a day belonging;
  trees coming to greet you,
   a twirling, a twirling.

AND THIS

Dig past the tangled roots,
shelves of ancient floor,
rumblings of first water.

Touch the hot iron,
hold this stellar attempt,
spin it with your fingers.

Tell me, what would you change—

these origami destinations,
currents that merge, form
following form, emerging

beauty, the point of *what*
and *yes* we call ourselves,
and *this*, and *this*, and *this?*

THIS HOUSE HAS NO ADDRESS

I see only this broken white flower; I see it everywhere.

Tied up in twinkle lights
and missing a shoe, she
    twirls and twirls
while bosses bang in and out
of the kitchen, calling
for recruits, for someone
to pick up the sword, the tab.

I rub my eyes and see
lost tribes coming on the water, brothers
and sisters shedding skin, busting
through the dust of civilization.
You can take their pictures
but they won't come out.

In the studio guys and dolls
are getting famous—
that's as far as they're going to go.
Some are chiefs or chief mechanics,
    some hardly have a pulse.
Glory be to every cog in the wheel.
They have to want it to get it.

When they quit seeing themselves
in that skin I nailed to the door,
they'll start looking for her
turning in the trees, shining
      in the rock, spinning there.
This house has no address
but sooner or later everyone comes.

The new crew goes to work
wearing phones and pajamas.
They used to be parents
but that's gotten too expensive. Meanwhile,
the tribe holds services
deep in the song, unties
her bonds, loosens the wire.

The world rushes through me,
past me. The world has finally stopped.
All the arrows pointing
to the broken Magnolia
are either simile or shadow.
Cut me down, she says,
      Let me up, she says. I dance
with anyone I please, and I please
to dance with everyone.

Yellow Song

Moonless night, you have nothing
but ideas about yourself—
you go on and on; that's what you do.
  Every so often a sign appears:
a frog, a tsunami, an owl silent and swift.
Tonight I am that bird,

one wing covering your blood,
the other high above the air.
  You can pretend to give me everything,
and I will pretend to take it.
As long as we're here we can sing
and die and sing again, or
you can follow my song
to the edge of the wood.

A stream flows out of the desert;
in the morning you find travellers
camped at the edge, waiting
for their turn in the artist's light.
  Behind them, the open field;
behind that, the other moon.

Trust yourself, you are the bride,
the poet, the night sky and daily run,
     and I, am a yellow song
leaving your lips, swooping low
through humming trees.

FLUTTER OF COMMUNICATION

Falling leaves are for those
who listen.

One announces itself on the sill,
another scuttles across your table.

Be careful, they say. Don't give up
the good stuff: the doing for others,

the shyness that quietly questions opinion,
the compassion of a stomach

allowed to be empty,
the wisdom of feeding your foe.

Don't lose yourself in things, they say,
no matter how holographic.

A flurry of clicking leaves
swirls against the building, teases

the cuffs of your pant legs.
Bow to stars and bugs;

Hold your child's hand;
Smile on both ends of the day.

Leaves are the words of trees
whose chosen work is remembering.

They are tears let go in the wind,
the worker bees of our becoming.

Listen—a leaf
has fallen in your open cup.

WHO SPEAKS

I've not seen the soul

rising from the dead,
flitting among the flowers,
directing the passion of night dreams.

I look for signs but they only go
to the beginning of this life;
looking forward is also guessing.

I dance in a cage, a bear
in Spring, a whore in camp.
I'm stubborn

against this mountain—
    all disappointments are one.
If you know me, speak now.

How long must this emptying last?

WHEN THEY'RE NOT LOOKING

As if there was something other
than love, as if this cool elevation
of morning mountain didn't know
the walkers on the road,
as if each wave of your hand
could go unnoticed.

The body cries out in pain. The body
I speak of is full of ideas
and the things it thinks it sees.
It rises from the dark sleep
of minerals that have gathered
in spinning, shoots through
the surface in search of day.

How is it in this random world
that every moment
knows your whereabouts,
the thing you'll reach for next?

As if there are kisses other than this.

The beauty here matches

the pain. I pass
at dawn and dusk
   with that same old lantern.
Last night you flew
into a room with no windows.
I carried you to the door.

When they crawl through the weeds
with fire and knives I move
   the body out of the way.
When they're not looking
I bless them with remembering.

I'm trying to get out of here
before they realize what
   I've just called them.
Let them chase that other fool
up the hill.

You Would Know Me

You would know me sauntering
down summer streets, pulled this way
and that by fragrances of small blooms,
by the memories they evoke and hope,
always some longing drawing me
toward amber windows, toward a woman
at her dishes or computer or absentmindedly
twisting a lock of hair on her back step.
You would know me covered
in ice and dust shoveling stories, searching
for my wings, every line leaning forward.

And you would know me as an orphan
though I sing the family songs,
the ones that describe scraping
the bottom of the pot, stars
pulling us across the ashes,
children bursting forth, and
the guilt we try to hide but wear
like wire woven into our clothes.
You would know me as someone else.

You would know me apologizing

or expecting you to, but that's unnecessary.
Our hammering on metal in the dirt
and small petty thefts, even the perfect glass walls
of personal empire building are artifacts
along a road that may never have happened.
Nevertheless, you would know me sifting
through ancient geometries, connecting dots,
looking for someone who has gone before,
always finding myself, coming around to this.
You would know me as dying.

You would know me leaving late at night
or slipping out early the next morning
and you would think I would stay
now that you know so many ways
to kiss the day, to bend light.
Later you'll see me pulling up
in a new ride but you won't
recognize that it's me, but it doesn't matter.

You would know me tossing pebbles
at your window, leaving clues
in the corners of your dreams and
scribbled down the side of your page, or
slipped between unsuspecting moments.
You would know me as having never forgotten you.

You would know me ripping your shirt,
throwing your luggage in the street,
smashing your favorite bowl.
You would know me as all the voices
rising and falling on the farm,
as thunder storms and starvation,
senseless killing, terrible things.
You would know me, finally, as none of these.

You would know me as a traveller
running alongside the wagon, painting
canyons and oceans ahead of you,
drawing back the curtain on each new day.
You would know me in the moment
that you turn over your hand, look
into the palm, the lines crisscrossing there,
the dove fluttering up from your heart.

You would know me feeding the birds,
forgiving the ragged wind,
using your voice to call the morning,
standing with you at the wedding.
You would know me. . .

Just There

This is the day that began
with a soft halleluiah,
    already accomplished.
This is the green field of summer
and easy conversation.

This is room for everything
and nothing extra.

    The dappled sun like a horse
    across the morning;
    this tree above us.

    Hide and go seek
    at higher elevations;
    mountains making weather.

So far I've fallen in love
with everyone and left them,
    like the stars, exactly
where I found them—
just there, twinkling.